RUBANK EDUCATIONAL LIBRARY No. 48

RUBANK

INTERMEDIATE

Method

T0079150

VIOLIN

LESLIE C. POTTER

A FOLLOW UP COURSE FOR INDIVIDUAL
OR LIKE-INSTRUMENT CLASS INSTRUCTION

HAL•LEONARD®
CORPORATION
7777 W. BLUEMOUND RD. P.O. BOX 13819 MILWAUKEE, WI 53213

Half step open to first – first to second

NOTE: Finger combination same as in the "Elementary Method for Violin" except whole hand is brought back.

Copyright MCMXXXVI by Rubank Inc.,Chicago,Ill.
International Copyright Secured

Finger Exercise

Finger Exercise

Name the notes. Pick out half steps. Note that B♭ and C♭ are half steps.

Play Ex. 1 in various bowings: ① W.B. ② H.B. ③ ④

Melody

Moderato

Count 1 2 & 3 4

Lullaby

Moderato

Brahms

Studies

Crossing the Strings

1st time: W.B. Grande Detache.
2nd time: M. to P.

1

2

3

4

Study in ⅜ time

Rhythm patterns: ① M. to P. ② N. to M. ③ ④ ⑤ ⑥ ⑦

5

Sweet And Low

Barnby

6

Moderato

Count 1 2 3 4 5 6

rit.

pp

Memorize melody and play in the rhythms.

Work out a few rhythms each lesson

Middle – point – nut

Staccato

Triplets
Bow at the point – m.- nut.

Syncopations

3 parts of the bow

Exercise to promote finger action

① (slowly)   ② ③ —Study daily.

Use above model for all strings. Keep fingers down.

"E"   "D"   "G"   etc.

etc.   etc.

Volga Boat Song

Russian

Moderato

Long slow bows — Expression and tone

Whole Steps

Study

Rhythms for this study:

La Donna e Mobile

Verdi

*Lively.   Think G#

Scale Exercises for daily drills
Study the diagrams and play in the various keys

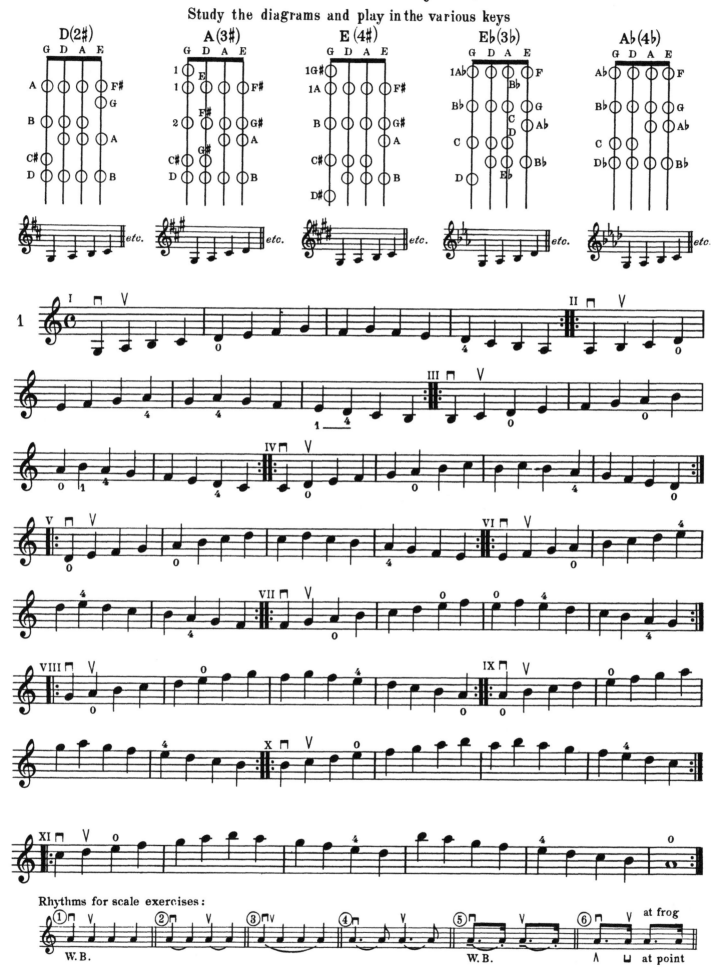

Rhythms for scale exercises:

Minuet

Mozart

Andante con moto

(D.C. = Go back to the beginning and play to the end without repeating the sections.)

Playing Tag

Allegretto
Pizzicato = pick*

Con arco = Bow

*Don't let the nail strike the string.

rit.

Study

Minuet

Haydn

Second Position

NOTE :
Teachers who prefer to start 3rd position first may turn to page 16 .

Crossing the Strings
Second Position

An Old Song

French

2nd Position Studies

Study Song

Scale Studies
Second Position

Bowings:

Practice this scale pattern in the following keys
Learn the names of the notes and pick out half steps:

LARGO from New World Symphony

A. Dvorak

*Play in the first position first.

Third Position
On one string

Play quarter notes:

Third Position

Crossing the strings

Bowings: ① ♩♩ ② ♩♩♩♩ ③ ♩♩♩♪ (quarter notes only.)

18

Annie Laurie

Home Sweet Home

May be played in 1st position first.

Bishop

Home Sweet Home
(Played an octave higher)

Tone study – Long slow bows

Scale Study in Third Position

Also practice in the following keys:

Remember these keys and the sharps and flats.

Bowings for Scale Study

W.B. W.B. H.B. M. to P.

Broken Chords

Play Ex. 1 in the following Bowings

Syncopation

① L.H. Bow — ② Upper Half Bow

Melody

Play in 1st position, then in third position.

Schumann

Study in crossing the strings

Memorize. Practice in 3 parts of the bow - middle - point - nut.

Slowly and Evenly

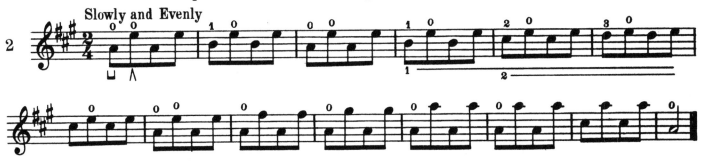

Practice now in the following rhythms

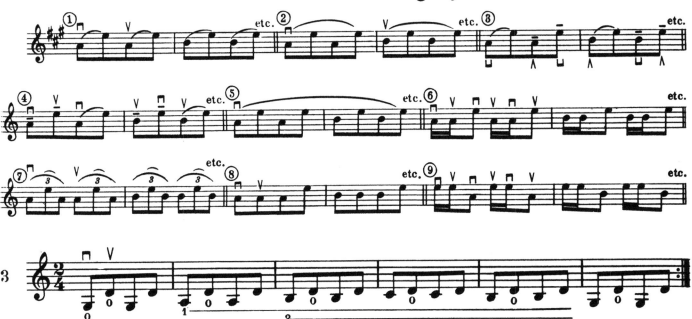

Study

Connecting the Positions
First and Second

*The first finger glides to the second position and then the second finger falls on the string (♩).

Exercises in 1st & 2nd Position

Play slowly and evenly

Andante

Dancla

＊ **Play in the first position first.**

Connecting the First and Third Positions

Using one finger, first using long bows, then slur

Using two fingers

Song from Oberon

Weber

Study

Crossing the strings

Minor Scales
1st and 3rd Positions

Study

Andante

Gluck

Allegro Moderato

Mazas

Andante

Intervals

Harmonics

Touch the string lightly with the fourth finger

Minuet

Beethoven

Finger Development

1st, 2nd and 3rd position. Play slowly at first.

Rhythms: ① ② ③

The Staccato

Study and perfect a few examples each lesson:

Down Bow at the Nut

*Place the bow on lower note and then draw the bow over the strings for the chord.

Crescendo Study

Study

Practice slowly first. Use various bowings.

Moderato

Minuet

Mozart

Trill Studies

With half steps (Play evenly and clearly):

With whole steps:

(♫ = Grace notes)

Andante

1st, 2nd and 3rd Positions

Allegretto
(Martelé Style)

Maestoso
(Broad singing style)

Thrown Strokes

Near the middle of the bow

Bounding Bow

Studies

The Spiccato or Springing Bow

The bow leaves the string by its own accord when the necessary speed is reached.   Do not try to force the bow to bounce.

Four notes

*Play No. 3 legato until fingers are firmly fixed.

Loure

* Best to count 1-2-3-4 first.

Bowing Study

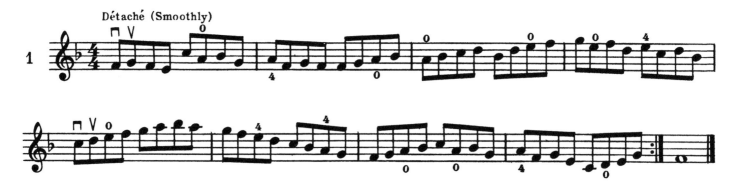

1

Rhythmic Patterns
(Variants)